AMAZIN
BIBLe STORY
mazes

Written by Laura Kelly
Illustrated by Joe Stites

Published by Shiloh Kidz, an imprint of Barbour Publishing, Inc.,
P.O. Box 719, Uhrichsville, OH 44683, www.shilohkidz.com

IN THE BEGINNING

Genesis 1-2

God made the sun, moon, and stars, and the earth with all its plants and animals. He also made a man named Adam. God gave Adam a very important job—naming and caring for the animals.

Draw a path to help Adam find the lost lamb.

THE TOWER OF BABEL

Genesis 11:1-9

Long ago, when everyone spoke the same language, people tried to build a tower to heaven. This angered God, so He made them all speak different languages. They never finished the tower because they couldn't understand one another!

Draw the worker's path to the top of the tower.

NOAH'S BIG BOAT

Genesis 6:9-22

God said to Noah, "The earth will be flooded with water, but I will save you and your family and two of every animal." God told Noah to build a big boat called an ark and to gather the animals. Noah obeyed.

Draw a path to help the animals find their way to the ark.

RAIN, RAIN, RAIN

Genesis 7

At last! Noah and his family and all the animals were inside the ark. Then it rained and rained and rained! God kept the ark safe as the earth was flooded.

Draw a path to help the little panda find her mate.

THE DOVE

Genesis 8:6-12

Noah sent out a dove to see if there was any dry land. The dove returned with an olive branch. This meant the treetops were above water. The water was going down! Soon, everyone would be able to leave the ark.

Draw a path to help the dove get back to Noah.

ABRAM'S MOVING DAY

Genesis 12:1-7

"Gather your family, and pack your things," God told Abram. "I have a new place for you to live." Abram obeyed. He knew God would take care of him and his family.

Draw a path for Abram and his family to get to the new land of Canaan.

THE COAT OF MANY COLORS

Genesis 37:3

Jacob had twelve sons. He loved his son Joseph most of all. One day, Jacob gave Joseph a special gift. It was a beautiful, bright coat of many colors.

Draw a path to help Jacob give Joseph his wonderful gift.

JOSEPH BECOMES A SLAVE

Genesis 37:4-36

Joseph's brothers were jealous of him. One day, they sold Joseph to traders who took him to Egypt as a slave. Joseph was very scared, but God watched over him.

Draw the path the slave traders took to Egypt.

JOSEPH'S FAMILY IN EGYPT

Genesis 39:2-6; 45:3-11

With God's help, Joseph became a very important man. When his brothers came to Egypt to buy food, they didn't recognize him—but Joseph recognized them! He forgave his brothers, and Joseph soon rejoined his whole family.

Draw a path to show the brothers the way to Joseph.

BABY IN A BASKET

Exodus 1:15-16; 2:1-10

The Egyptian king, Pharaoh, ordered that all Israelite baby boys be killed. One woman put her baby in a basket and placed it in the river. A princess found the basket and named the baby Moses.

Draw a path to help the basket reach the princess.

"LET MY PEOPLE GO!"

Exodus 3:1-10

One day when Moses was grown, he saw a burning bush. God spoke to Moses from the flames. He told Moses to go to Pharaoh and tell him to let the Israelites leave Egypt.

Draw a path to help Moses deliver God's message to Pharaoh.

Exodus 14:13-31

When the Israelites left Egypt, Pharaoh decided to chase after them.
At the Red Sea, God divided the waters, and the Israelites crossed safely.
But the water came down upon the Egyptians.

Draw a path to help the Israelites cross the Red Sea.

THE TEN COMMANDMENTS

Exodus 20

Moses went up a mountain to talk with God. There God gave Moses a set of rules for His people written on two stone tablets. These rules were the Ten Commandments.

Draw a path to help Moses take the Ten Commandments to the Israelites.

THE WALLS CAME DOWN

Joshua 6:1-21

God told Joshua and the Israelite army to march around their enemy's city, Jericho, while the priests blew horns. They did this for six days. On the seventh day, God made the walls of the city crumble.

Draw a path to help the Israelites march back to camp.

SAMSON THE STRONG MAN

Judges 14:5-6

God gave Samson super strength so that he would one day be able to battle the Philistines. As a young man, Samson used his might for the first time when he fought a ferocious lion!

Draw a path to help Samson find the lion.

SAMSON'S SECRET

Judges 16:4-22

God told Samson to never cut his hair—it was the source of his strength. But Samson told Delilah his secret, and she told the Philistines. They cut his hair, and Samson lost his mighty strength.

Draw a path from the Philistines to Samson.

RUTH AND NAOMI'S JOURNEY

Ruth 1

Naomi's husband and sons had died. "I am going back to Bethlehem," Naomi told Ruth, her daughter-in-law. Ruth hugged Naomi and said, "I will not leave you. Your people shall be my people and your God, my God."

Draw a path to lead Naomi and Ruth to Bethlehem.

A KING IS CHOSEN

1 Samuel 16:1-13

Samuel was a prophet. God sent him to the house of a man named Jesse. "One of Jesse's sons will become king of the Israelites," God said. It turned out that the future king was the youngest son—David!

Draw a path to show Samuel the way to Jesse's house.

DAVID AND GOLIATH

1 Samuel 17:17-24

One day, David was sent to take food to his brothers at the army camp. When David got there, he saw that the soldiers were afraid of Goliath, a giant Philistine from the enemy camp.

Draw a path to help David get to the army camp.

DAVID SLAYS THE GIANT

1 Samuel 17:45-50

David went to face Goliath with only five stones and a slingshot. "I fight you in the name of the Lord!" David shouted. He fired his slingshot, and the stone hit Goliath's forehead, striking him down with the might of God.

Draw a path to help David find Goliath.

SOLOMON'S TEMPLE

1 Kings 6

David's son, King Solomon, built a wonderful temple. Then Solomon and the priests and elders filled it with holy treasures. They did this to honor God.

Draw a path to help Solomon place the treasure in the temple.

FED BY RAVENS

1 Kings 17:2-6

There was no rain in Israel for many years, but God made sure the prophet Elijah had enough water to drink from a small brook. He also sent ravens with meat and bread for Elijah to eat.

Draw a path to help the ravens find Elijah.

A POOR WIDOW'S FAITH

1 Kings 17:8-16

God sent Elijah to a town where he met a very poor woman. She only had a small amount of flour and oil to make bread with, but she shared it with Elijah. God made sure her flour and oil never ran out to reward her faith.

Draw a path to help Elijah reach the poor widow.

CHARIOT OF FIRE

2 Kings 2:1-11

One day, Elijah was walking with his friend, Elisha. Elijah was old and tired and finished with his work as a prophet. God sent a chariot of fire to separate the men, and He took Elijah up to heaven in a whirlwind to live with Him forever!

Draw a path from the chariot of fire to Elijah and Elisha.

HEALED IN THE RIVER

2 Kings 5:1-14

Naaman, a mighty Syrian soldier, was very sick. "Bathe in the Jordan River seven times," the prophet Elisha said. Naaman did and was healed!

Draw a path to help Naaman get to Elisha and the river.

THE HOT, HOT FURNACE

Daniel 3

A king threw Shadrach, Meshach, and Abednego into a fiery furnace because they hadn't worshipped a gold statue. An angel protected them, and they were not burned. The king then praised God and welcomed the men out of the furnace.

Draw a path to lead Shadrach, Meshach, and Abednego out of the fiery furnace.

DANIEL AND THE LIONS' DEN

Daniel 6

Daniel prayed to God even though it was against the law. When he was caught praying, King Darius had to throw his friend into a den of lions. God sent an angel to close the lions' mouths. The next day, the king was happy to see Daniel was still alive.

Draw a path to help David out of the lions' den.

THE BEAUTIFUL WIFE

Esther 2:1-18

King Xerxes wanted a wife. He had the most beautiful women in the land brought to his palace. When he saw an Israelite girl named Esther, he asked her to marry him.

Draw a path to help Esther get to the king's palace.

JONAH AND THE GIANT FISH

Jonah 1-3

God ordered Jonah to go to Nineveh and preach to the people there. Jonah tried to run away, but he was thrown into the sea. Then God sent a big fish to swallow him! After three days, the fish spit Jonah onto shore. Then Jonah obeyed God's command.

Draw a path to help Jonah get to Nineveh.

THE ANGEL'S MESSAGE

Luke 1:26-33

The angel Gabriel told Mary that she would have a very special baby. The baby's name would be Jesus. He would be the Son of God, and His holy kingdom would never end.

Draw a path to guide Gabriel to Mary.

Luke 2:1-7

Mary had to travel to Bethlehem with her husband, Joseph. Bethlehem was crowded—all the inns and houses were full. Mary and Joseph found a stable and decided to stay there. That night, baby Jesus was born.

Draw a path to help Mary and Joseph find the stable in Bethlehem.

GOOD NEWS!

Luke 2:8-15

The night Jesus was born, shepherds nearby were watching their sheep. Suddenly, an angel appeared and told them the good news. "You will find Him lying in a manger," the angel said. The shepherds hurried toward the city to find the baby Jesus.

Draw a path to guide the shepherds to the stable.

THE WISE MEN

Matthew 2:1-12

In a faraway land, wise men saw a bright star in the heavens. They knew it meant the King of kings had been born. After a long journey, they found Jesus. They worshipped Him and gave Him gifts.

Draw a path to help the wise men get to Bethlehem.

IN MY FATHER'S HOUSE

Luke 2:41-48

One day in Jerusalem, Mary and Joseph realized that Jesus was missing. They searched all over and found Jesus speaking to the temple teachers.

Draw a path to help Mary and Joseph find Jesus.

JESUS IS BAPTIZED

Matthew 3:13-17

When Jesus grew up, He went to the Jordan River to be baptized by John the Baptist. The Spirit of God came down on Him from heaven in the form of a dove.

Draw a path from the dove to Jesus.

START ▶

●STOP

FISHERS OF MEN

Matthew 4:18-22

Jesus walked by the Sea of Galilee. He saw some fishermen. "Come, follow me," He said, "and I will make you fishers of men." Peter, Andrew, James, and John became Jesus' first disciples.

Draw a path to guide the fishermen to Jesus.

THE LITTLE BOY'S LUNCH

Matthew 14:13-21

A little boy came to hear Jesus speak. He offered his lunch to help feed the crowd. When Jesus blessed the boy's five loaves of bread and two fish, there was suddenly enough to feed 5,000 people!

Draw a path to help the little boy reach Jesus.

THE GOOD SAMARITAN

Luke 10:25-37

Jesus told a story about a man attacked by robbers. A priest and a Levite passed by the hurt man lying in the road but didn't stop to help him. Finally, a Samaritan stopped, put the hurt man on his donkey, and took him to an inn.

Draw a path to help the good Samaritan find the injured man.

THE GOOD SHEPHERD

Luke 15:3-7

Jesus said that God is like a good shepherd who loves all his sheep. A person who disobeys God is like a lost sheep. God rejoices when a disobedient person comes back to Him, just as a shepherd rejoices when he finds a lost lamb.

Draw a path to help the shepherd find his lamb.

THE PRODIGAL SON

Luke 15:11-32

A young man had wasted all the money his father had given him. To survive, he had to take a job feeding pigs. One day, he decided to go home, but he was worried that his father wouldn't want him back. His father gladly forgave and welcomed him home. God is like that father.

Draw a path to lead the young man home.

JESUS BLESSES THE CHILDREN

Luke 18:15-17

"He's too busy. Go away," the disciples told the people who brought their children to Jesus. "Do not stop them," Jesus said. "Let the little children come to Me. The kingdom of God belongs to ones like these."

Draw a path to show the families the way to Jesus.

THE LAST SUPPER

Luke 22:7-37

Jesus sent the disciples Peter and John to prepare a supper. While they ate, Jesus told His disciples that this would be His last meal with them, and that He would soon face a great trial.

Draw a path to help Jesus and the disciples get to the Last Supper.

THIRTY COINS

Luke 22:1-6; 23:23-25

For thirty silver coins, Judas, one of Jesus' followers, led the temple guards to Jesus. The guards took Jesus to the temple priests. They decided that Jesus must die!

Draw the path that Judas and the guards followed to find Jesus.

HE IS RISEN!

Luke 24:1-8

Early Sunday morning, three women went to Jesus' grave. The stone in front of His grave had been rolled away! An angel appeared and said, "Jesus is not here, He is risen!"

Draw a path to help the women return home and spread the good news!

START

STOP

ANSWERS

page 7

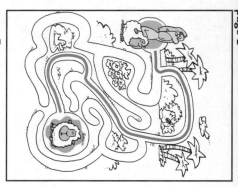

page 6

page 12

page 8

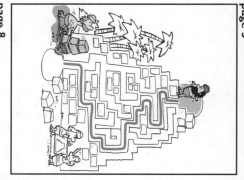

page 5

page 13

page 9

page 4

page 14

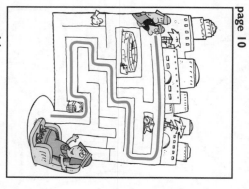

page 10

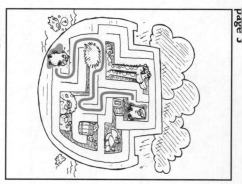

page 3

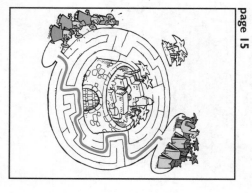

page 15

page 11

page 6

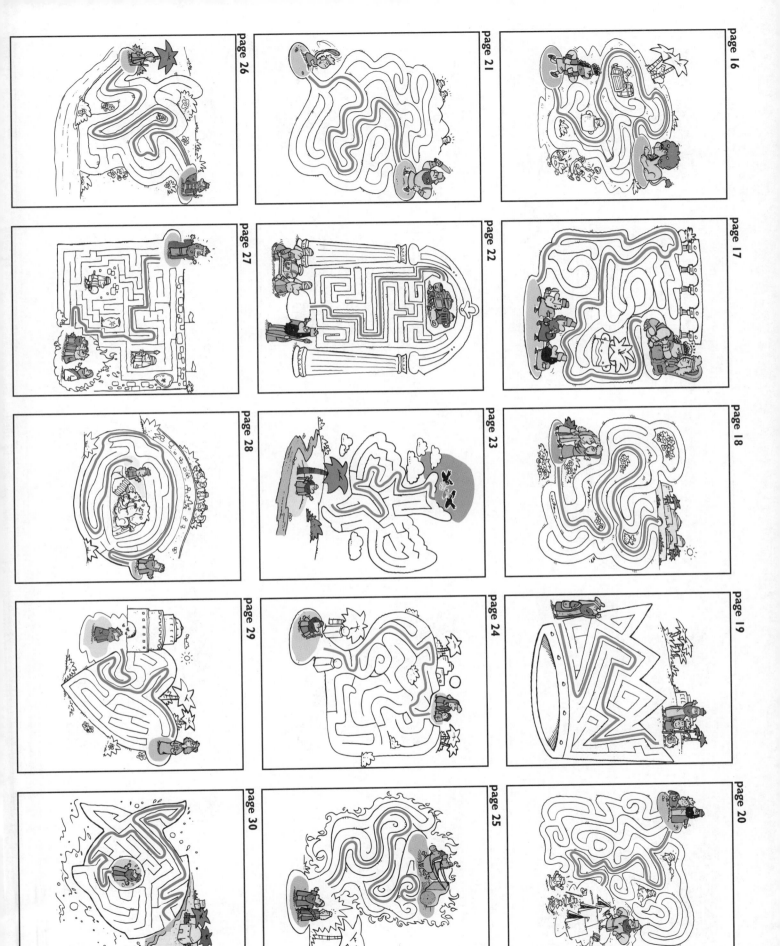

page 16

page 17

page 18

page 19

page 20

page 21

page 22

page 23

page 24

page 25

page 26

page 27

page 28

page 29

page 30

page 31

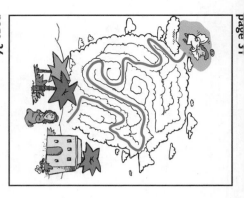

page 36

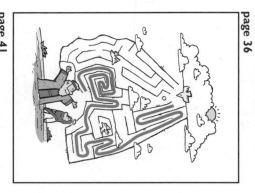

page 41

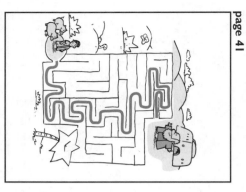

page 32

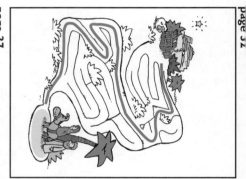

page 37

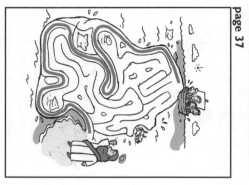

page 42

page 33

page 38

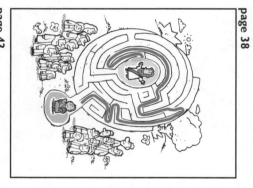

page 43

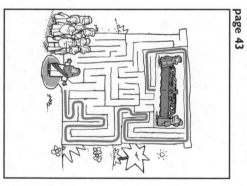

page 34

page 39

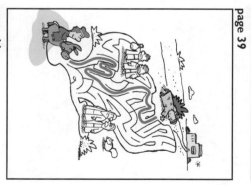

page 44

page 35

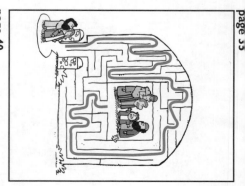

page 40

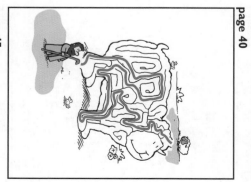

page 45